poems and
pictures of

light
love
life

poem	theme
tiny stars	universe
temple dogs	childhood
a beautiful game	fun
budleigh salterton	joy
beautiful love	love
cinquains	intimacy
snake	spirituality
air	dominance
war poem	conflict
the soul of a whale	nature
rosemary	family

written and illustrated by thurston jones

isbn : 978-1-80049-874-7

Tiny Stars

The Evening sky,
Too bright, for us.
We lie and watch,
The stars solace.
Waiting.
Soft,
blindness.

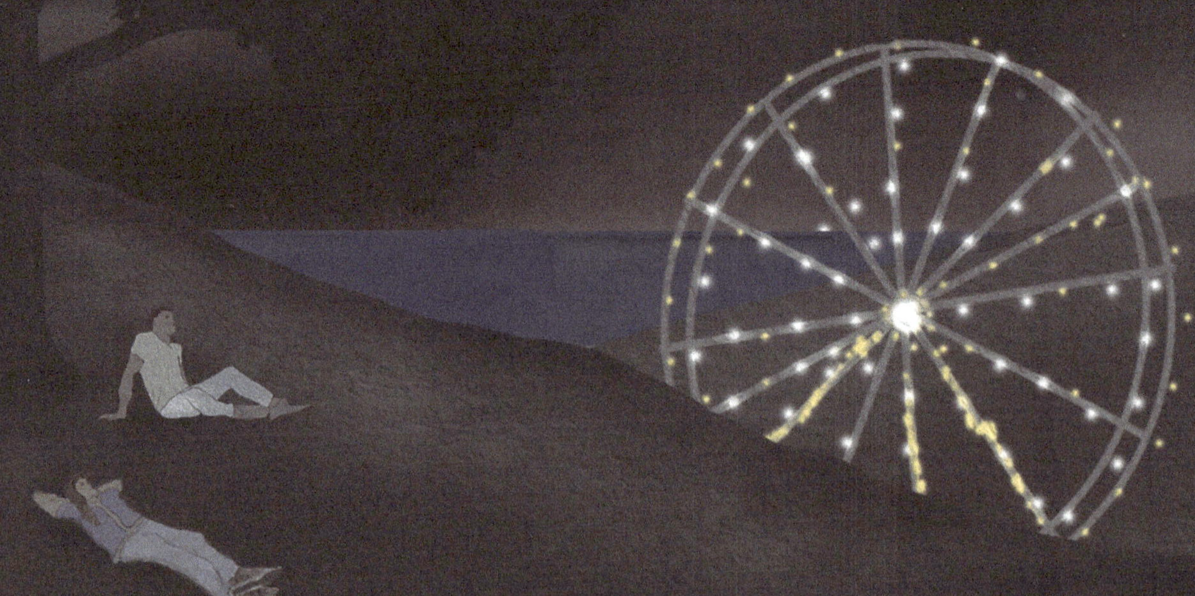

Fairground flutes,
Strings snap a stare.
Small lights address,
To create affair.
Smiling.
Sound,
calmness.

No peaks or troughs,
Too slow for kites.
Now moving still,
This waxing sprite.
Floating.
Slight,
lightness.

By TV aerial,
Elevate our eye.
Through clouds above,
We begin to rise.
Receiving.
Night,
darkness.

Above tranquil seas,
Intent for stars.
Over city lights,
This glow of ours.
Flying.
High,
boundless.

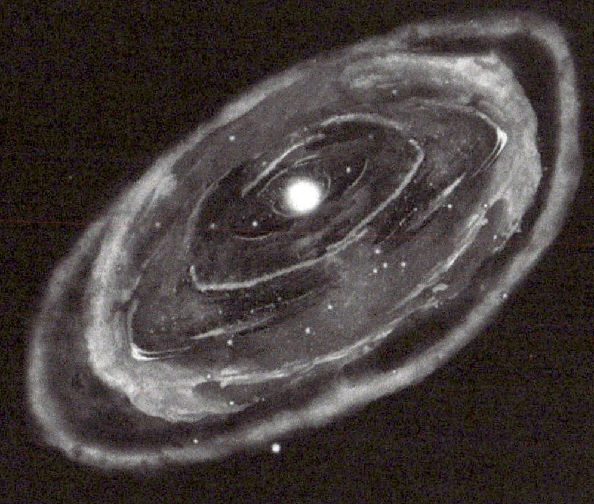

Our eyes they yield,
Void from all grace
Of reflective sand,
In celestial space.
Gazing.
Wonder,
brightness.

Temple Dogs

The sun's rays woke each dog at dawn.
First, Maya to open an eye;
then Taow, flicking a tail at flies,
and Kwan is last to crack a yawn.

The temple has always been a home,
for any stray that ceased to roam.
To stay a while and belong;
as long as they all get along.

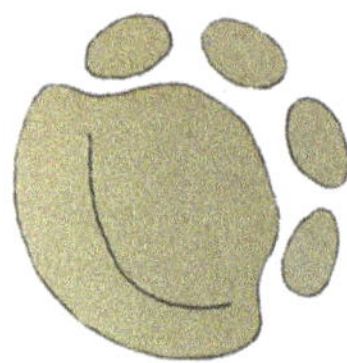

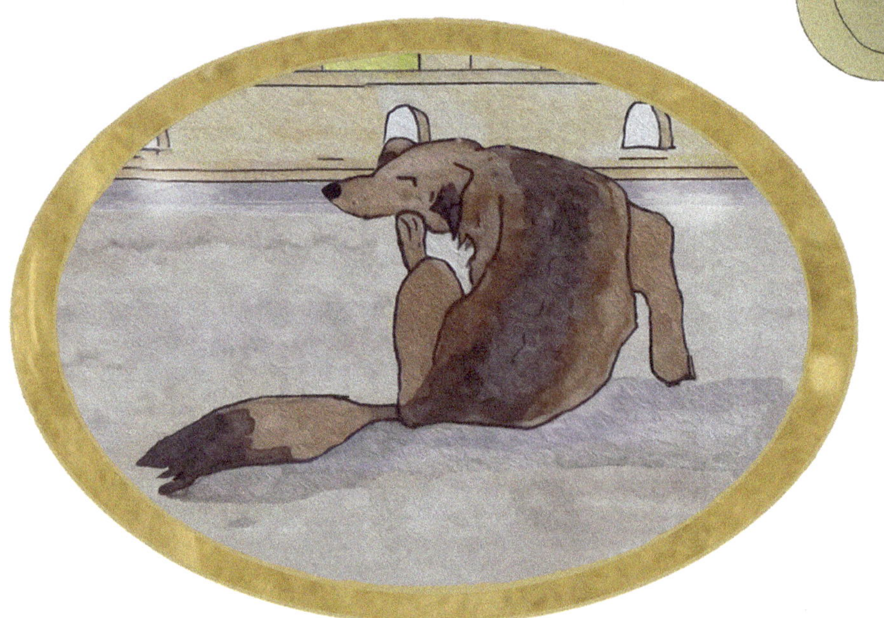

The market is the place to go,
a healthy start for little Taow.
Chasing rickshaws along the way;
getting stronger with each day.

Now, one place where dogs get their kicks,
whilst chasing tails and chewing sticks;
Is splashing through the ocean's spray,
cool soggy-sand is great for play.

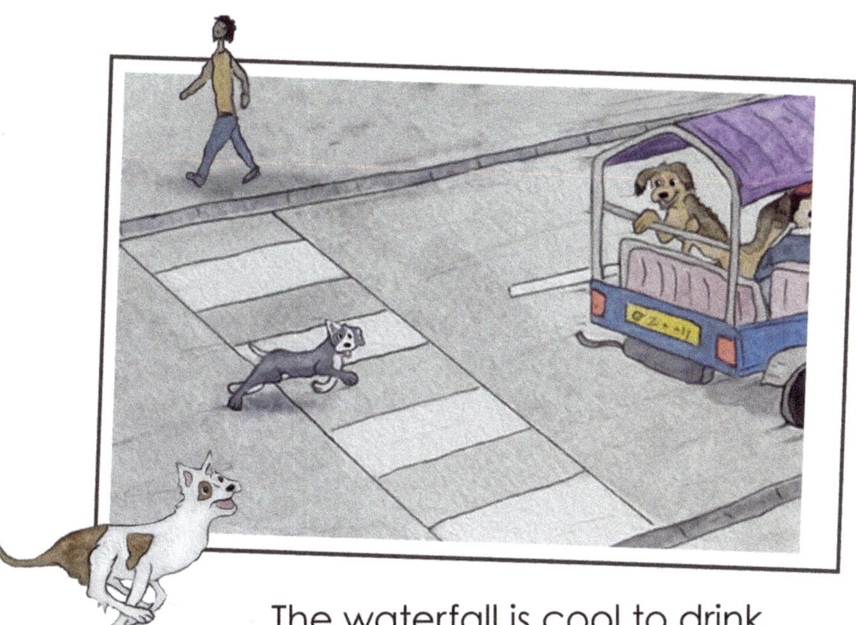

The waterfall is cool to drink,
and dampens down a salty taste.
A passing elephant fills its trunk,
then blasts them clean with just one grunt.

All freshly bathed, they head for town.
With empty tums, their supper waits.
Kwan begs for food with nudging nose;
whilst Maya cleans up all the plates.

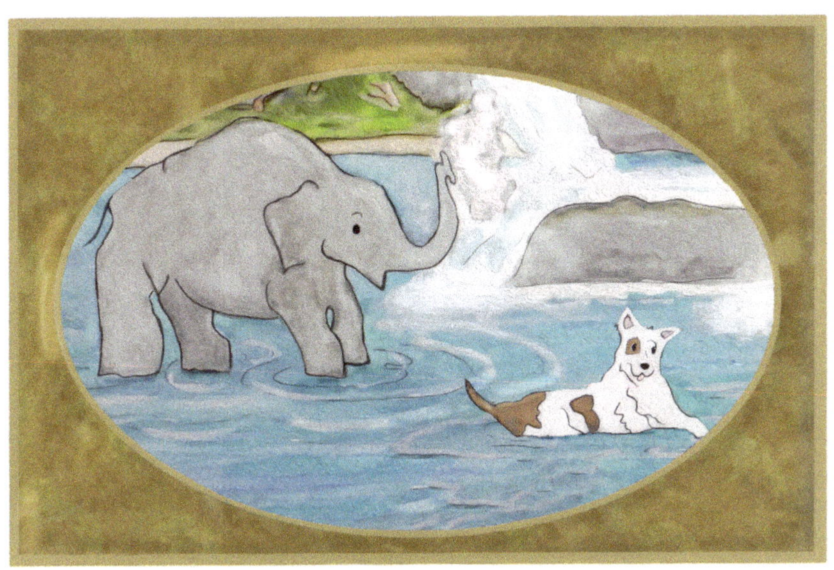

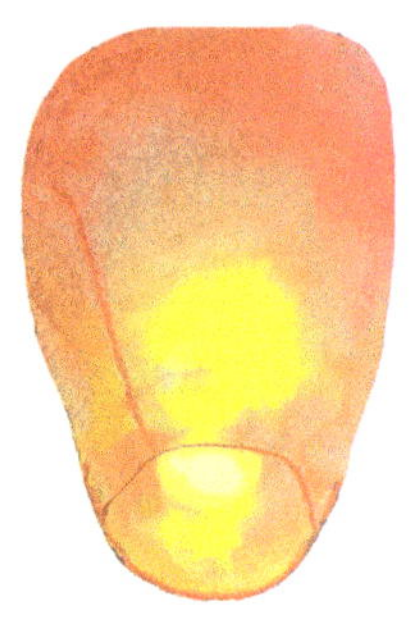

A place to settle from lonely roads,
is in a doorway close to home.
Curled together to feel so close;
the rustling leaves start their doze.

The sun has fallen far from us,
and melts within the evening's dusk.
Small specks of light burn into the night,
whilst legends from the stars arrive.

Free to dream of the boatman's tales,
without the wind of bellowed sail.
Gliding towards the night sky stream;
past moonlit stones and black ravines.

Up here, temples glow across the lands;
volcano's smoke like chimney clouds.
Our temple dogs begin to woof,
as strays howl sweetly to what's above.

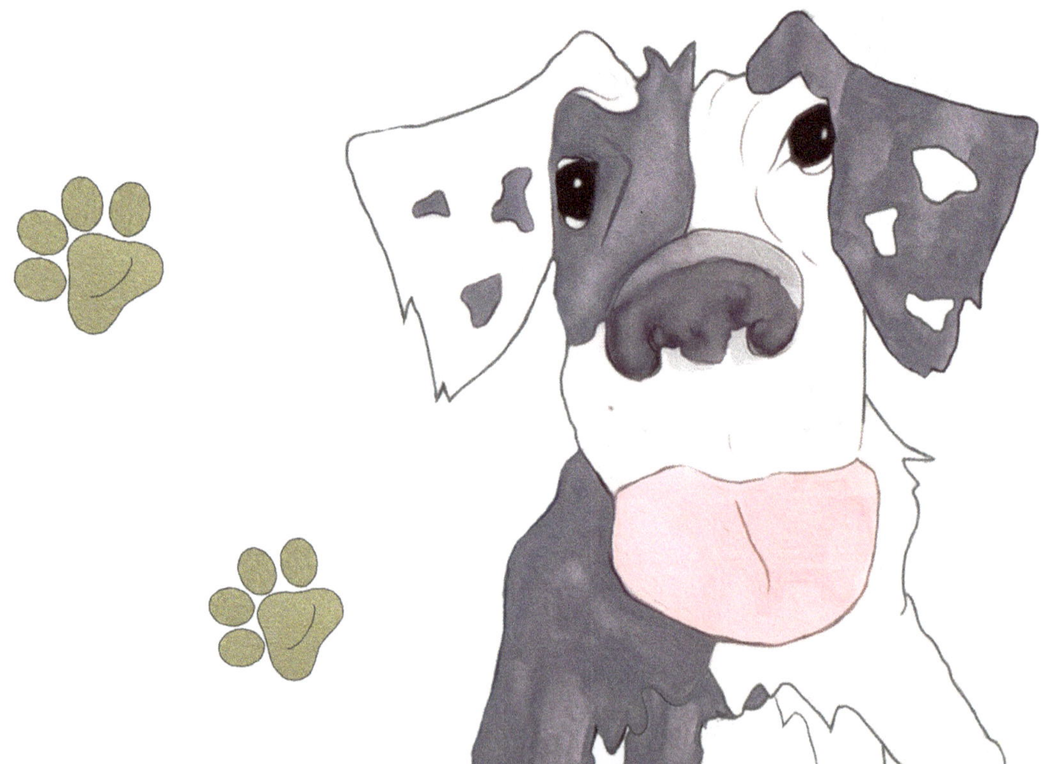

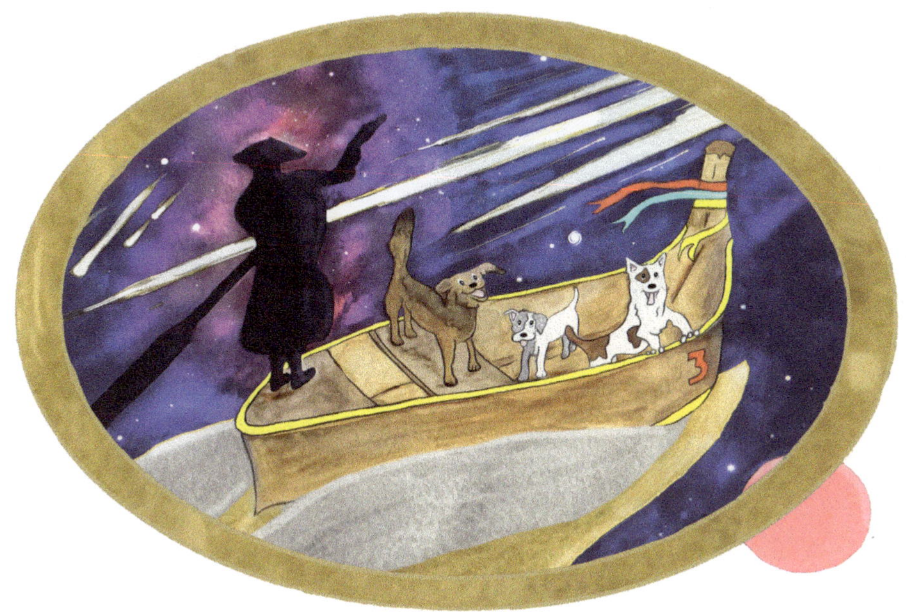

The sparkled stream begins to flow,
through clouds of glitter, the boatman rows.
To galaxies and shiny moons,
then back to home the long-boat zooms.

The sun's rays woke each dog at dawn.
The boat, now gone. As Maya's first;
to open an eye back down on Earth,
and Taow and Kwan begin to yawn.

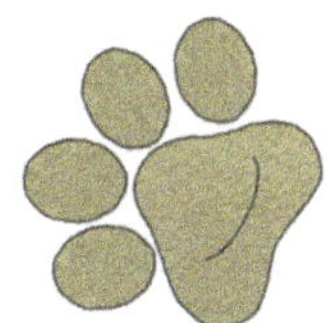
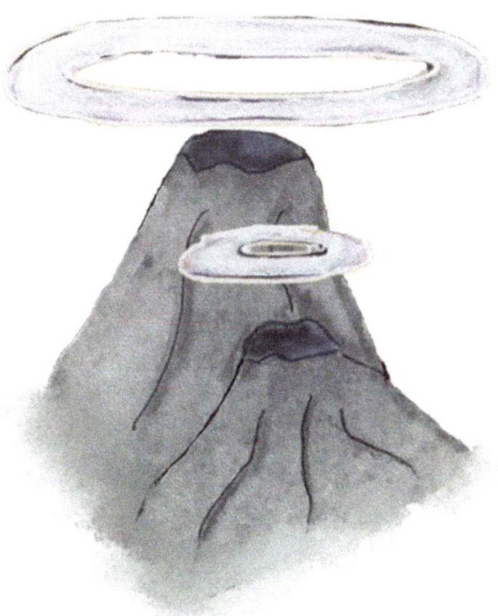
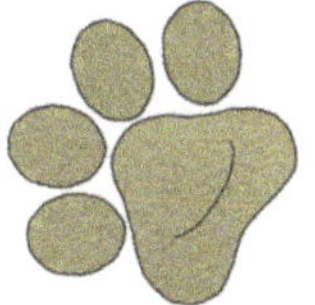

A Beautiful Game

Gotta handful of football stickers;
In my pocket an old tennis ball.
We'd meet up in anticipation;
for footie on the way back from school.

Anyone is welcome to play;
there's a field in each Albion town.
Meeting folks that you may not remember;
if alone, then why not come down.

We would carve out a pitch for the play,
dropping blazers, rucksacks and coats.
A briefcase alongside, if you're lucky;
dumped down for a couple of posts.

The goal was sized by the ages
of the keepers who kept guard within.
The pitch by the numbers of players,
from embankment to recycling bins.

Sometimes in the dust of the gravel;
along kerb of a warm, tarmac road.
In green fields, longing to play on;
the smell of cut grass on our clothes.

The ball was blasted up high;
that speck just visible by eye.
Until it came back down to greet us;
sometimes being trapped on a thigh.

The clatter of scampering feet,
of a knockabout down in the park.
The tackles on bruised ankle streets;
from a kickabout just after dark.

Second Half

Flicking the ball on shoe leather,
to hit the tight corner of goal;
was often dependant on pressure
of the ball that you're trying to control.

Some shots were lost in the hedges;
better ones bouncing off walls.
The odd ones smashing far windows;
all from the poor pass of a ball.

Some shoes were better than others;
as gravel punched in thin soles.
One or two had their favourite colours
but we all wore trousers with holes.

The crosses had been coming all year.
Most, with fascinating ease.
When jumpers explode, there's cheer
whilst lauding our man's qualitites.

Our position gave no detriment;
nor losses or injuries known.
No biased opinions amongst us;
an identity of which we still own.

A kick about by the bus shelter;
some footie played in your work break.
Maybe practise some skills by yourself,
to show off when you see your old mates.

Budleigh Salterton

Falling through the tumbling dunes,
down to the coolness of the tide.
Slant our hips towards the sun,
start spinning stones towards the sky.

Some flopping, many skimming.
Each dap, each time, each bounce.
Some plopping, all are sinking;
far tap, far line, far count.

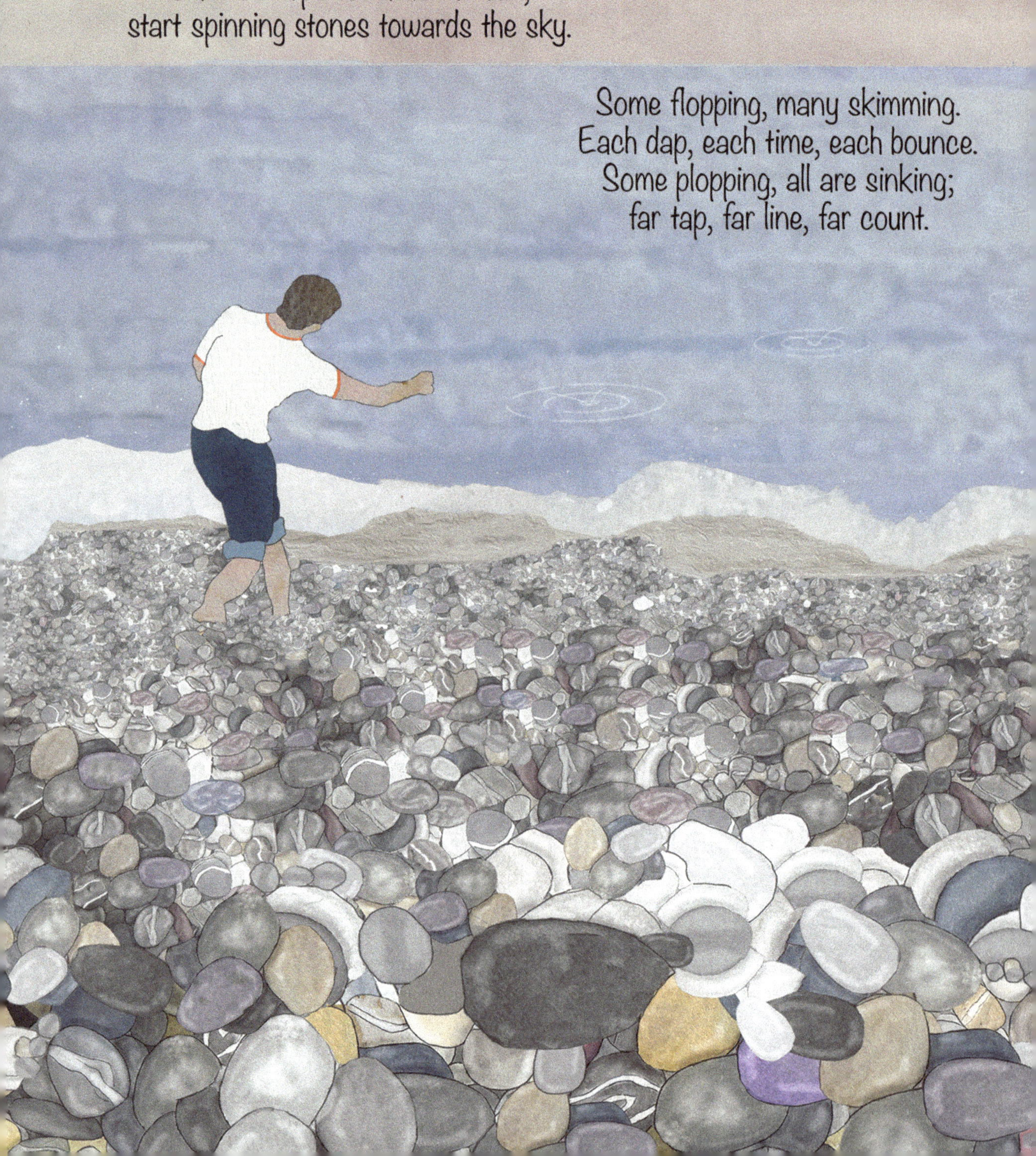

Closer now, the reaching waves
through shingle flowing scupper.
It's only then you come alive;
rich stars, in scars of colour.

I don't know why I chose you
from all the pebbles that are spun.
Shy of height, as others few;
sat plump, right in my palm.

The tide remains on repeat calm;
long furrows swallow dotted stitch.
I flip you up and watch you fall;
Slap- then slip you in my pocket.

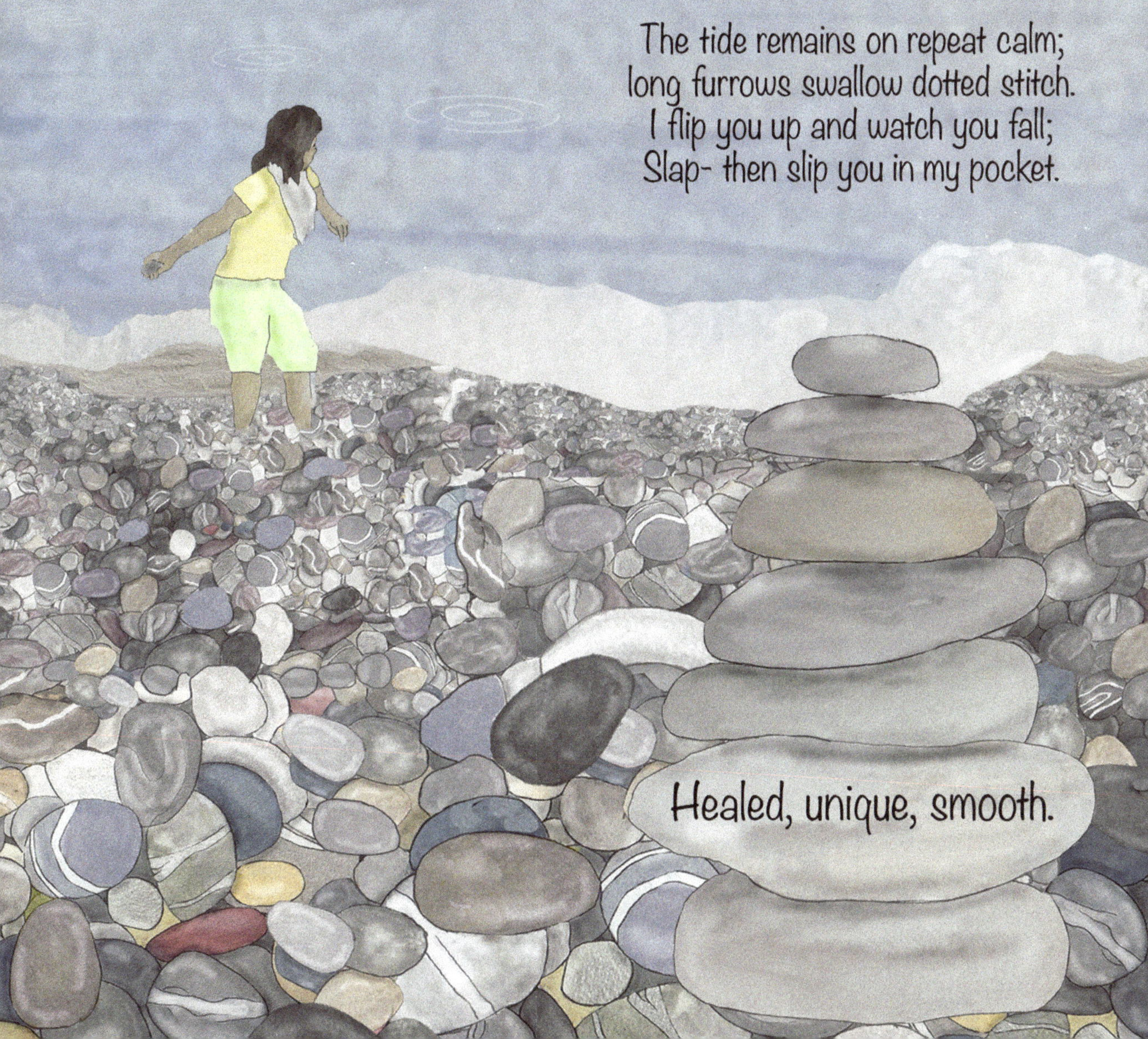

Healed, unique, smooth.

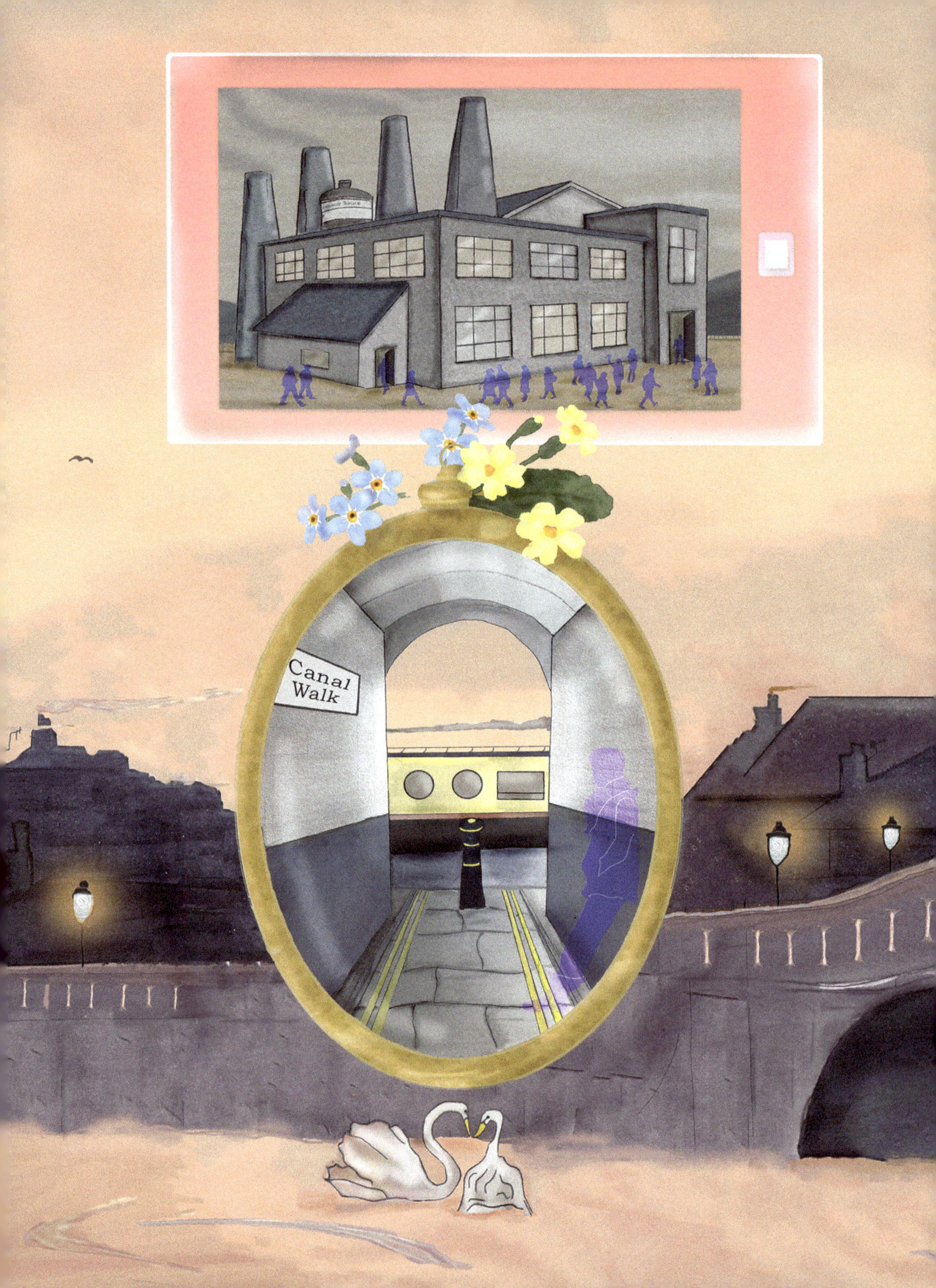
Canal
Walk

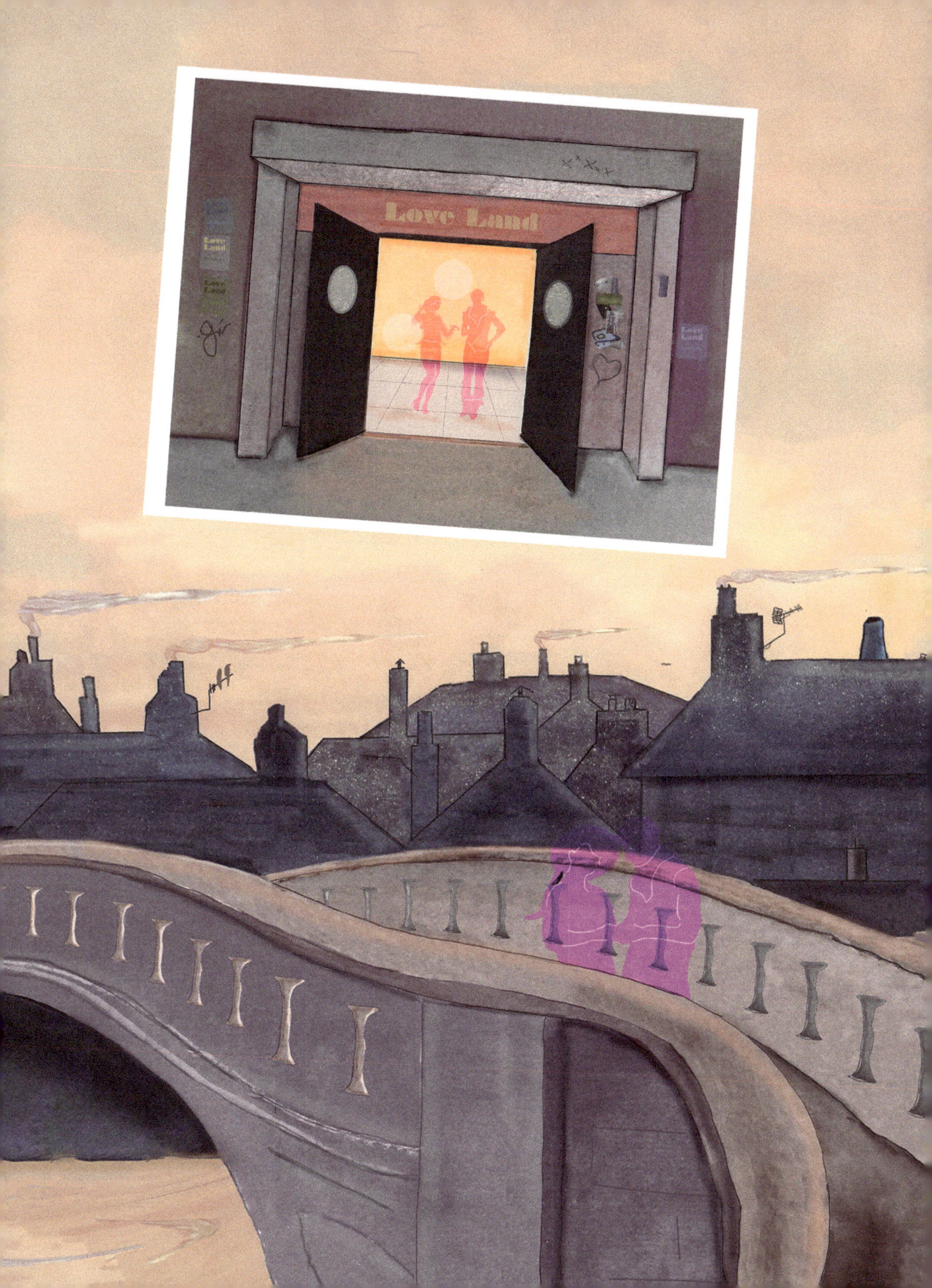

Love Land
Love Land
Love Land
Love Land

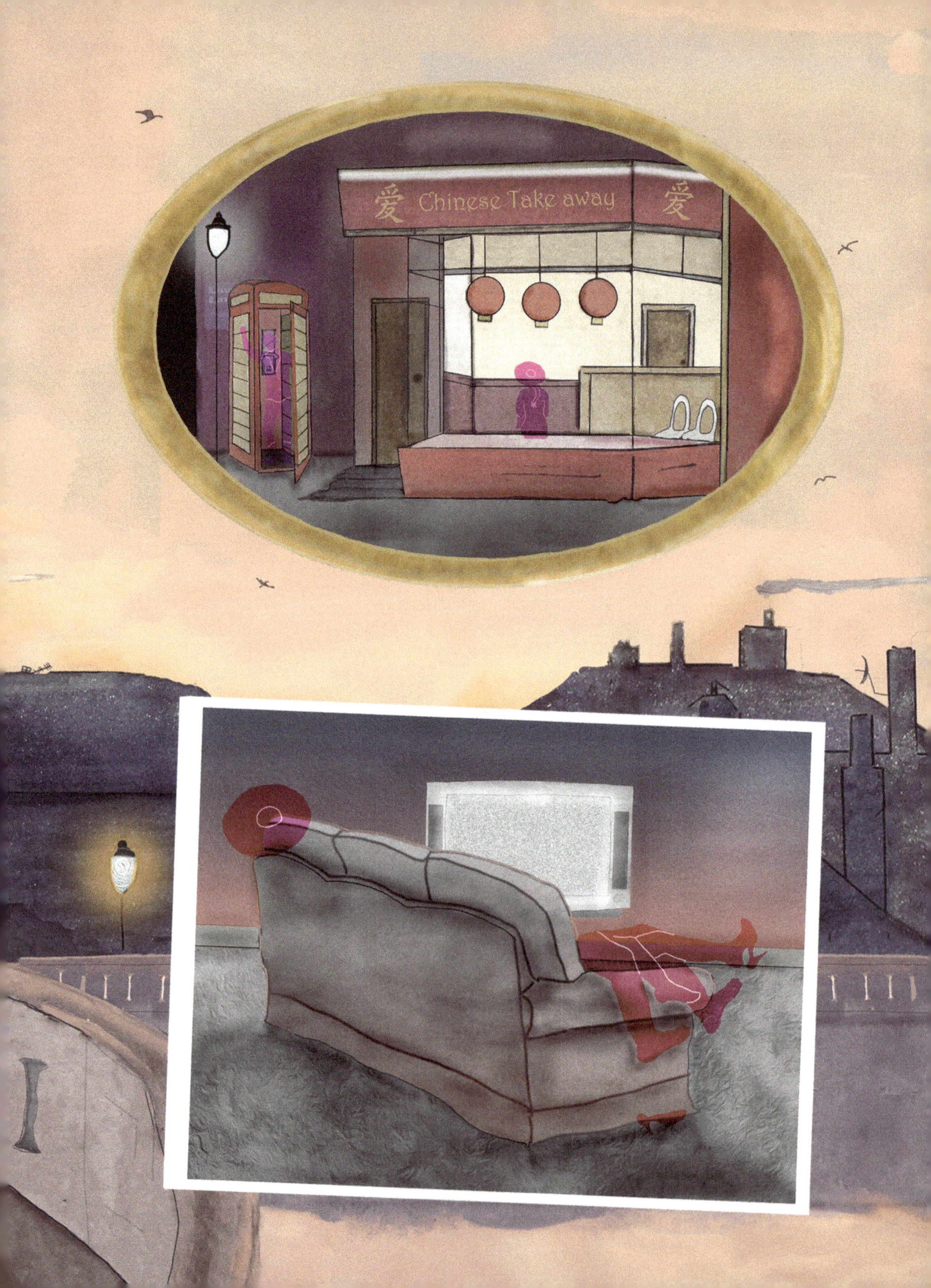

Chinese Take away

Beautiful Love

Morning sun, for it's time I know;
unveil our eyes, I'll have to go.
All goodbyes are left unsaid;
work bell calls from the road ahead.

I'll see you when the siren calls;
I'll be leant against the passage walls.
Through waving hands, sash and boots;
from crowd, your smiles flicker through.

I'll warm your hands on bowing bridge;
over pastel swirls on smokey ridge.
By peachy swans entwined for life;
nuzzled by draughty doors arrive.

You hold my waist and dance so slow,
at social club then picture show.
With drinks and friends, the hours few;
a joyful promise yet to prove.

Fluorescent noise and hanzi signs;
from window seat to waterside.
Embrace tin foil in plastic bags.
Hail from the cold, a taxi cab.

To lounge settee and late tv;
a place of wild divine so be.
I swear on every bond and vow;
our eyes engage until times allow.

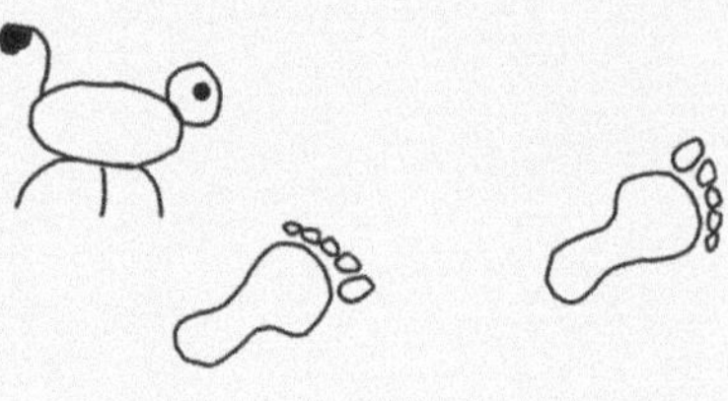

Flip flops;
jumping on rocks;
steady me without socks;
along that slippy waterfall;
one June

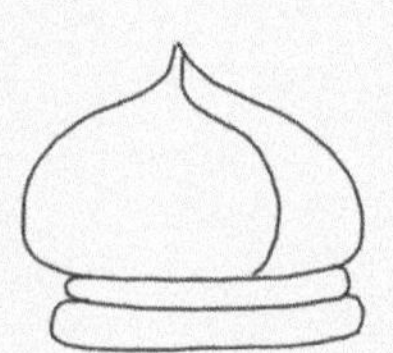

Agra.
We eat, drink, smoke.
Evening settles day's dust
Tales of a french woman, machines
and Orchha

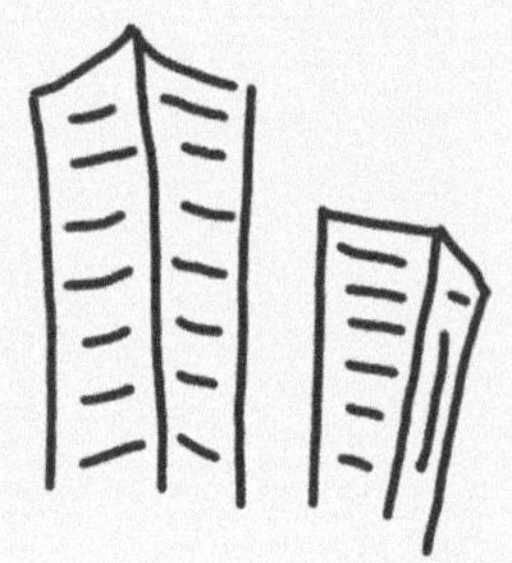

Cab ride;
city at night.
In the back curled up tight,
just stargazing at skyscrapers
with you.

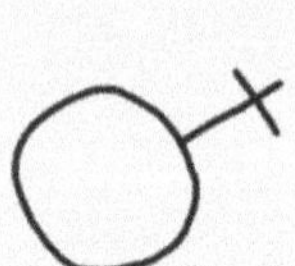

So close.
This airport room.
I know its our last night
but a moment, so sad to say,
goodbye.

For you.
This afternoon,
one hundred placed kisses.
Later one hundred placed kisses
from you.

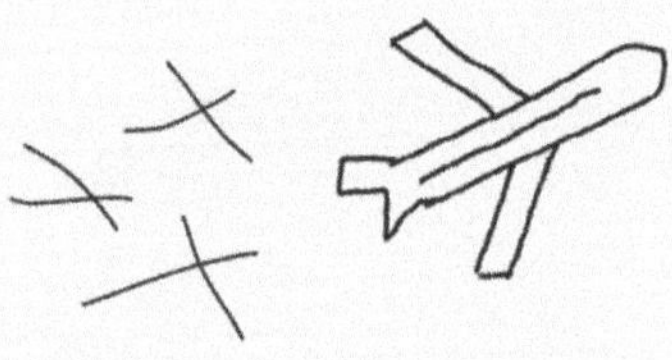

Midnight.
Down river's rise
in a shopping trolley.
Without hestitation you pushed,
laughing.

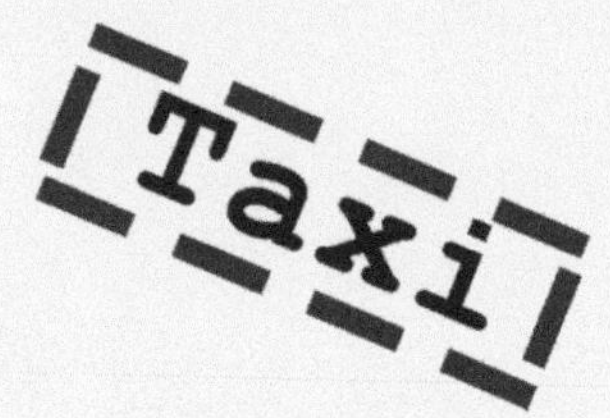

Taxi!
Smiled, side-saddle,
politely agreed fare.
I step away from the spectrum;
you've gone.

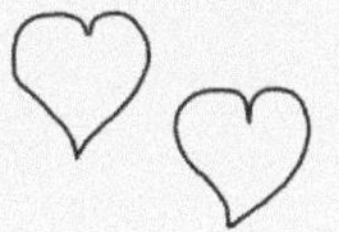

Caress.
Each piercing glance.
Give all to the moment.
Your deep, warm heart turns to kiss me.
Lover.

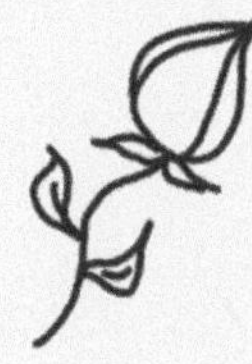

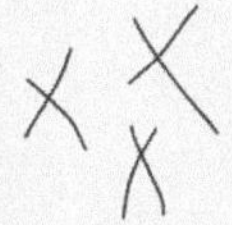
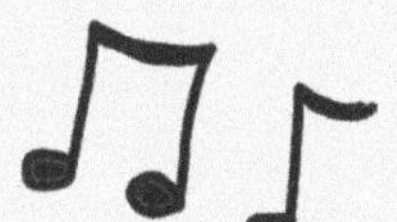

Moonlight;
you on the bars.
All alone and in love.
Just us singing the 'Lost Highway'.
Rollin'.

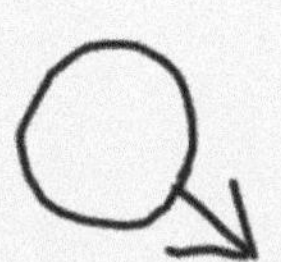

Once more,
from train to train.
Holding hands we just fit;
from Bond St back to Marble Arch.
Doors close.

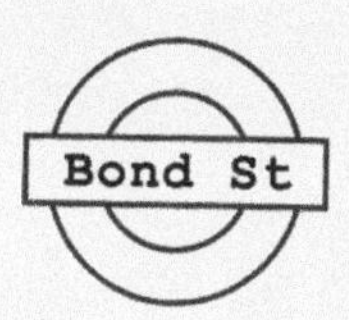

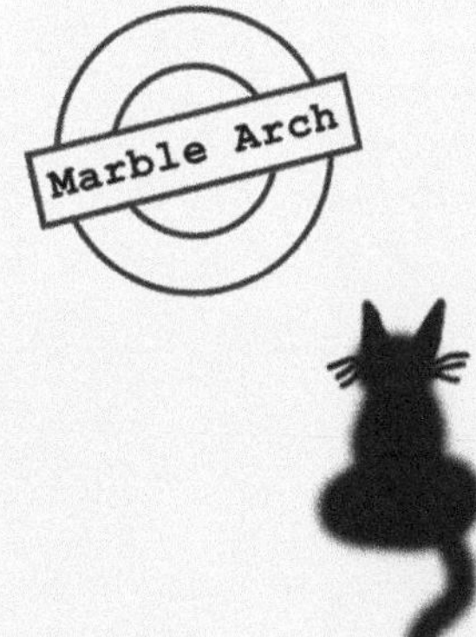

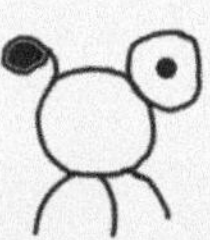

Our time.
Just you and me.
Stroke away that dead fur;
grooming my ally's neck and ears.
Purring

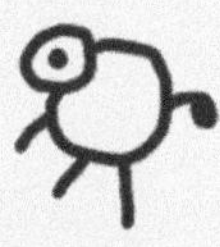

Space

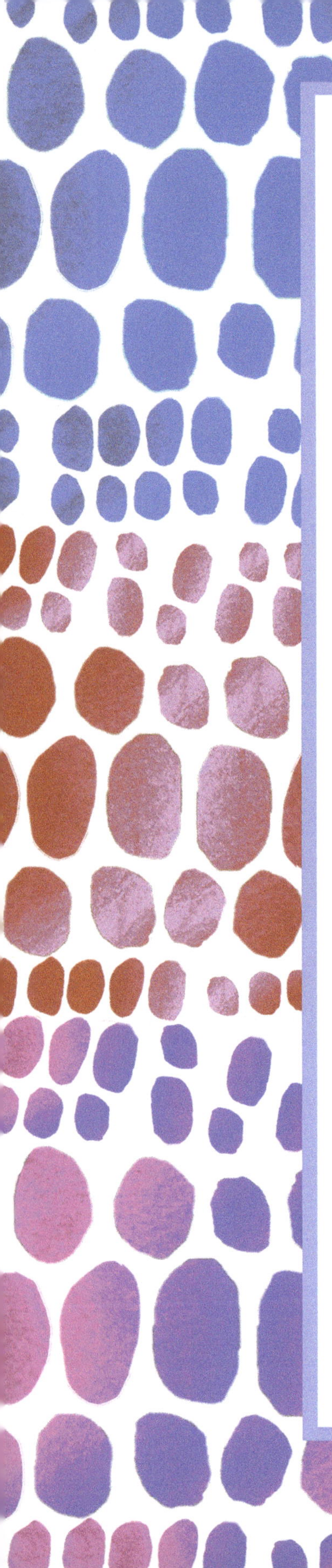

Snake

I have spent my time,
crawling through life's dirt.
Creeping in gutters;
a tough skin beneath
sequins of colours.

You all know me;
close to the ground.
So rarely seen,
since time began.

Stay the same
within - whilst
shedding skin.

Tasting
the sky.

Sss.

Sliding
through sand.

Beneath stones;
diving seas;
coiled from trees.

Only at night;
venomous strike!
Squeezing the life;
cold blood delight.

Spiritually
unclean. Yet I feel
all, everything but
how I wish for the
soul of the eagle.

air

in the air
you are there
surrounding me
knowing
around me
always

faint wispy clouds
accompany me
each day
i am reminded
of the times
of your dark
clouds

you are always
there
i don't wish
for these days
only days when
you're not near
just clear skies

War Poem

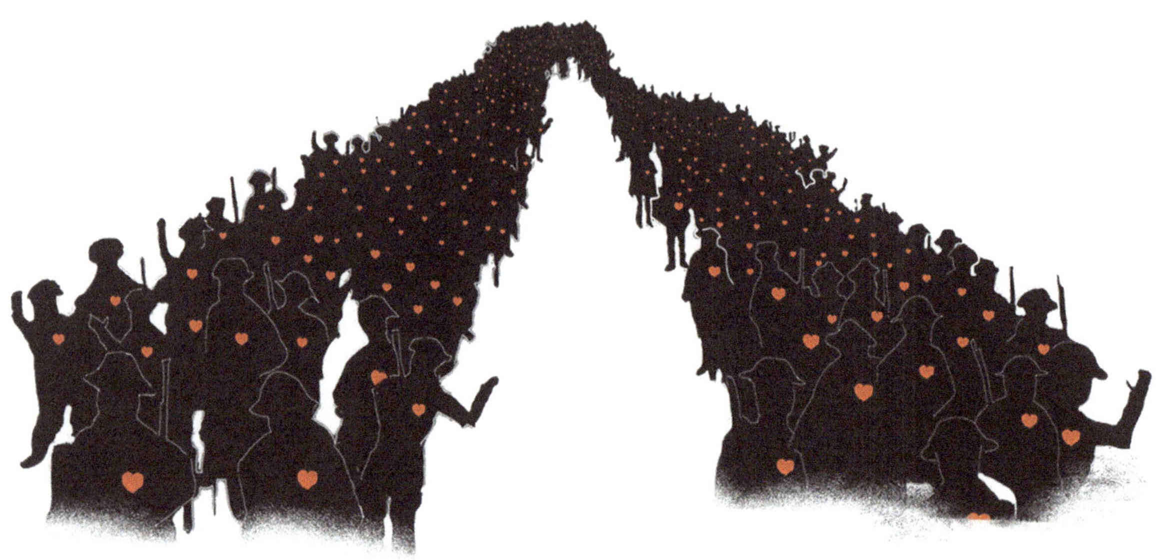

Spring carried its call
on that May morning;
amid churning the fields,
to felling the pine.
Each homage affirmed,
enlisted in prime,
and they marched into War
without warning.
Singing deep from within
to their strides of rhyme;
"The light in our hearts
is the source that consoles.
Love warmed all
and each one of our souls."

Now, nailed within
this rat hole to skyline;
paced, black-splintered stumps;
shot-blown and laid low.
From that charcoal far line,
a shadowed halo;
a speed-throbbing sound
started coming.
The outbreak of fire
rapped dark clay on below.
Scorching and tearing
the raw nerve of the fierce;
through hung, fleeting clouds -
the same vista appears.

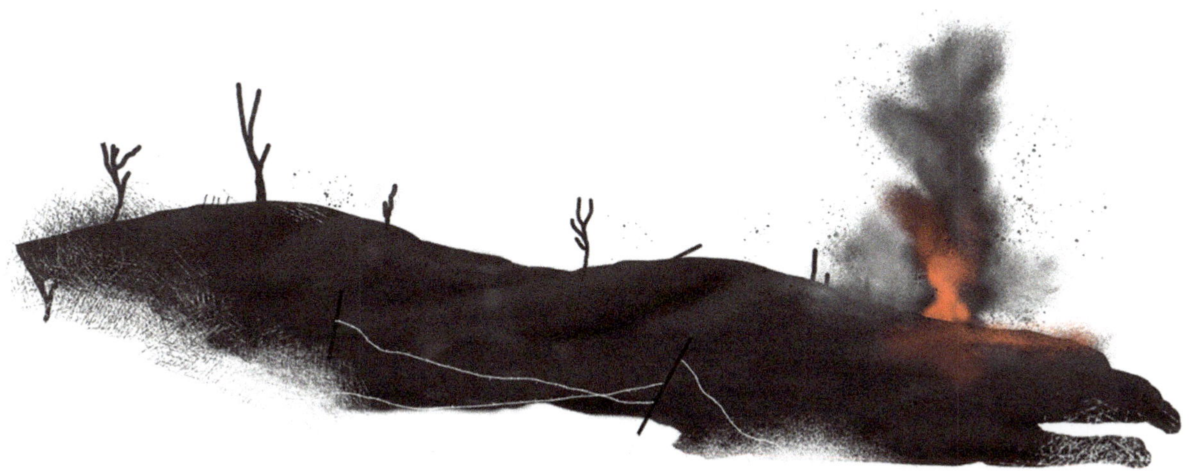

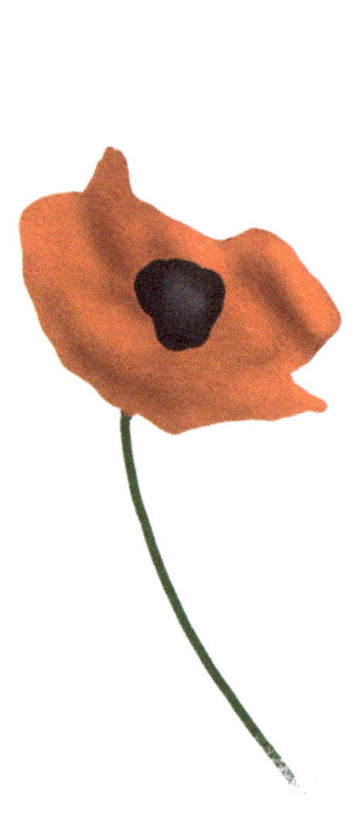

Shells scattered the prey,
some froze there like stone.
Bodies laid pardoned,
no senses to mind.
On thrashing forty twos,
each man was descried,
til' cruel furnace heat
levelled each one alone.
Raged on, piercing white
to shatter inside;
as courage's flame,
cools soft with the breeze.
For this time known now, is just memory.

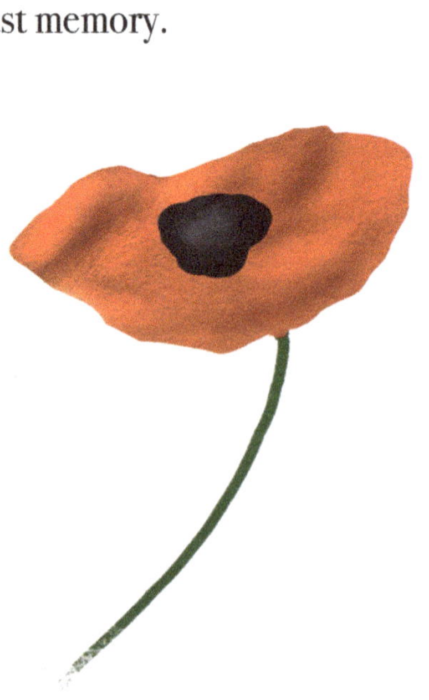

"Oh star of night
will you guide me to thee.
I never paid mind
of your shine until now.
Lucid you are,
in that black-river. Crowned;
Far from frozen Earth
that now drains me.
May we be gone! Radiant,"
on muttered prayers.
"In life; far from time.
Oh, when will it be?
When all Man′s love, lights
this world for us to see!"

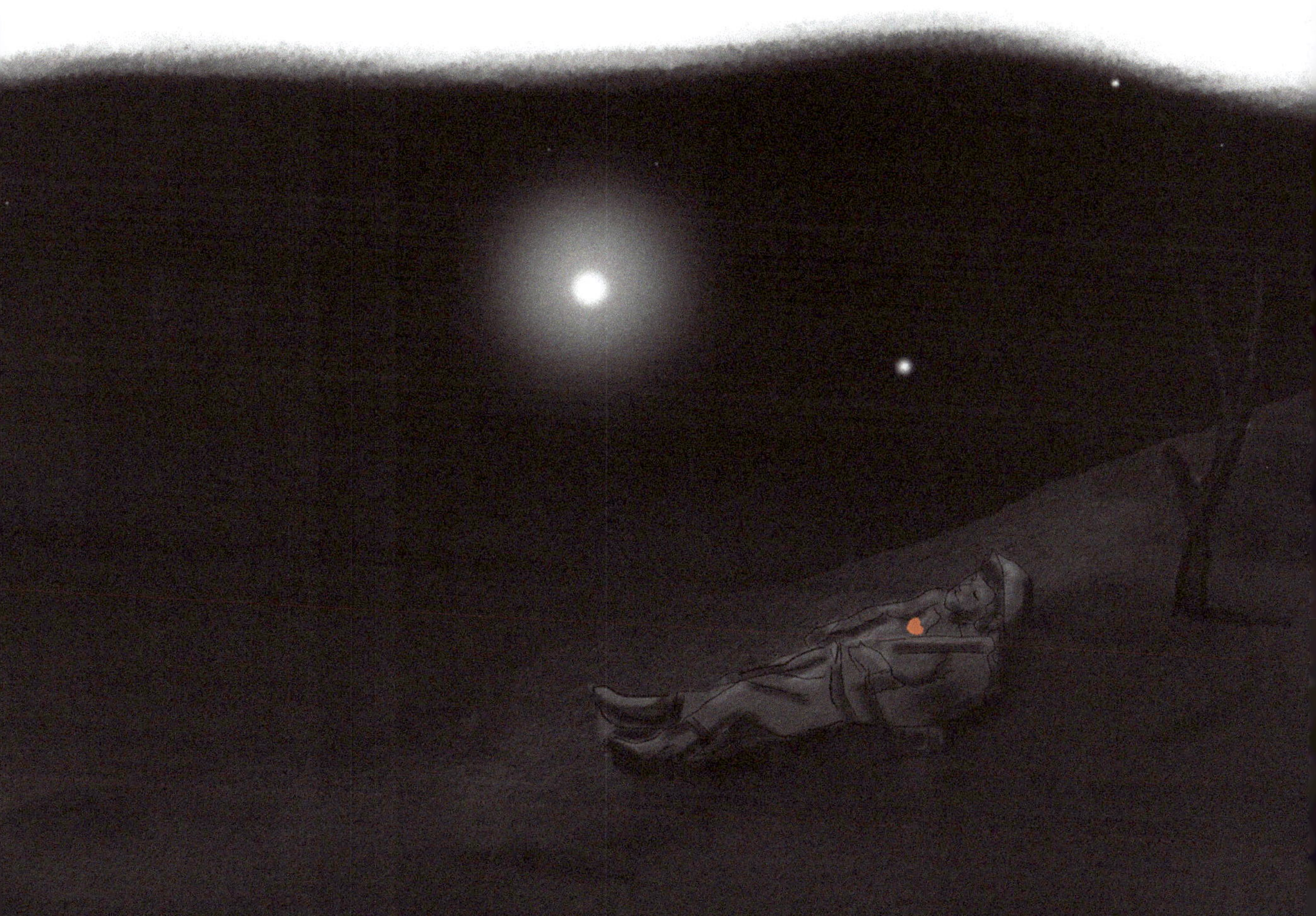

The Soul of a Whale

Awakened. In-between a dream
and the cool, blue breeze.
A breeze that rushes through these pleats;
enlivening these senses .
Truly alive through the blues
of every shade and hue;
No matter how wild these waves become.

The great pleasure of movement;
all life supported by ocean.
Delighting the senses of the mind.
Rushing from dark depths to sparkled skies;
Engulfing, enormous mouthfuls
of seawater, the taste like a human's tear.

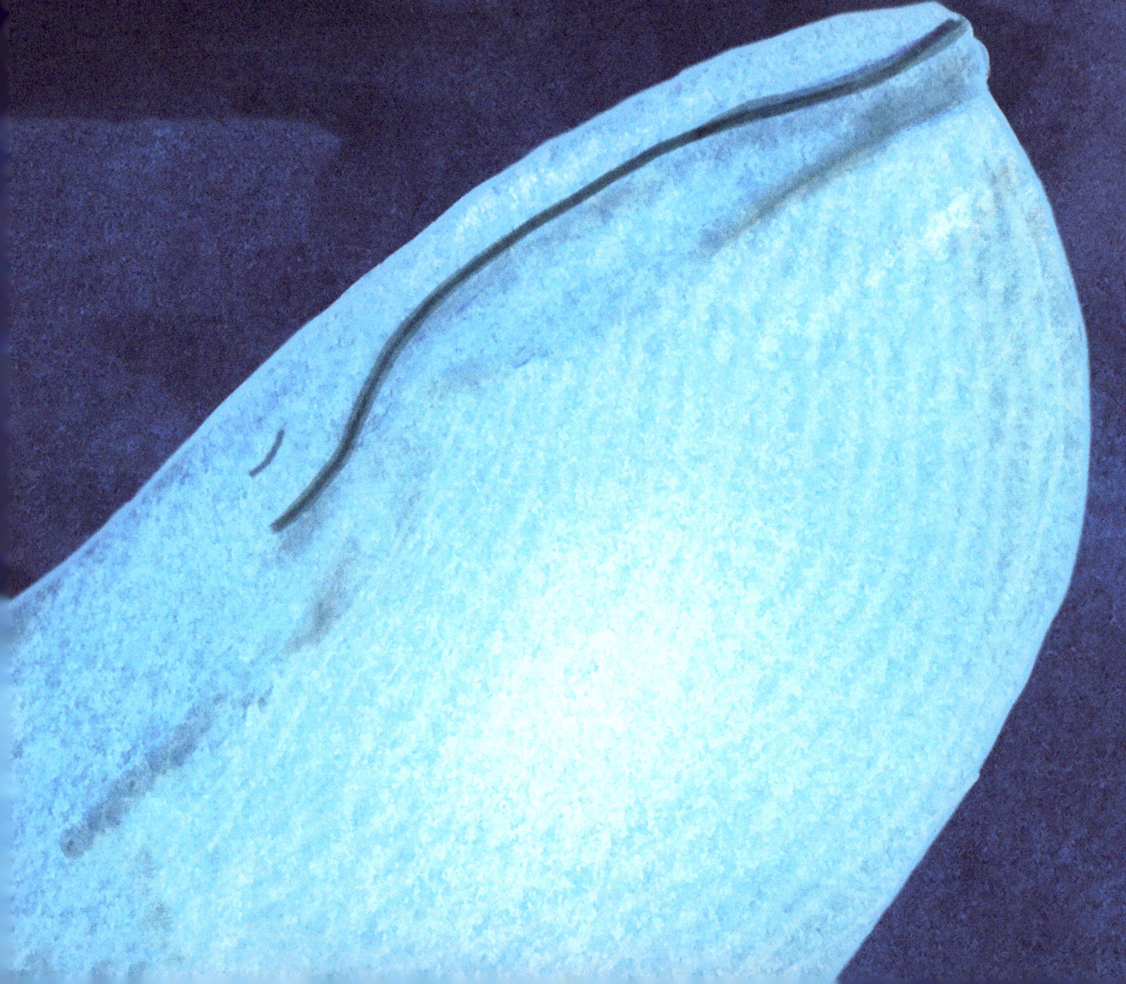

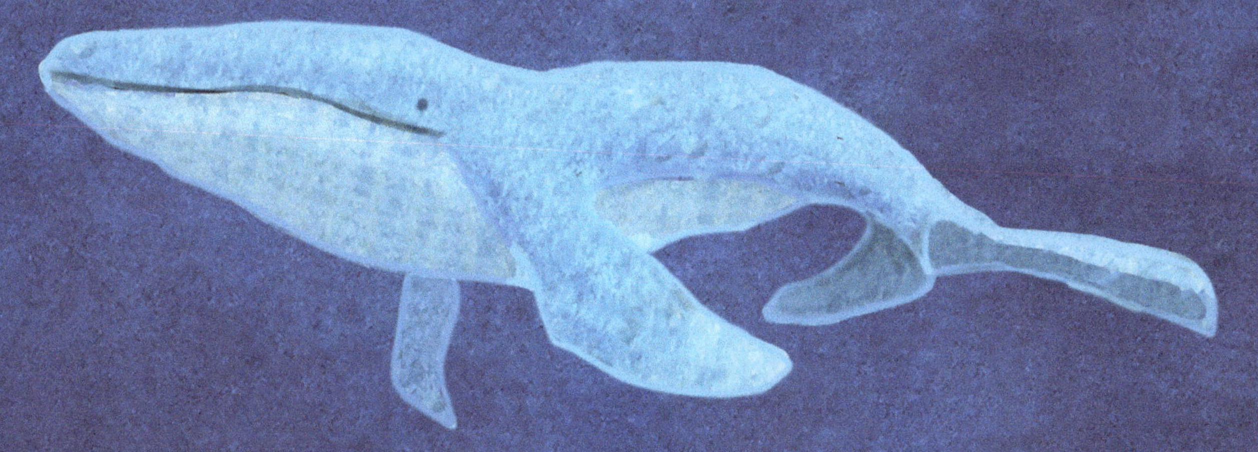

Across thousands of miles she glides
with the certainty of distance
and satisfaction of her sounds.
A beauty far from a concept
yet a reality born by the stars.
It is in everyone of us,
everyone who dares to dream.

The embodiment of character
and her spiritual nature,
lies above all features and traits.
Like every man, woman and child,
freedom is all and everything.
Unique, yet not solitary,
for she has a calf in tow.

Man may never infiltrate
the unfathomable soul of a whale.
Given to her, the greatest gift
that nature bestowed on any
mammal.
A truth that is unknown except
by a divine revelation.

Rosmary

The sun shined on us all that day;
your agile mind and graceful smile.
It's true, you were adept and strong,
as you walked your daughter down the aisle.

Those bitter winds keep spinning leaves;
both up and down these frozen streets.
A speech now shrouded in the unknown.
To kindly neighbours, you are alone.

The summer shines whilst you rest,
on o' lime sofa that you still own.
As blue, masked folk call by and care;
you watch cbeebies in your new home.

Today, we've smiles from hanging nets
and in brown eyes, your warmth for life.
However strange these times become,
you'll always have us by your side.

Tomorrow, you'll peep about the curtain,
as I drop my boy around for you.
Forever, days played in your garden;
are just in albums for you to view.

This week, you've gazed through open window
whilst holding tightly to the drapes.
Whenever frustrations do occur,
remember there's laughter that awaits.

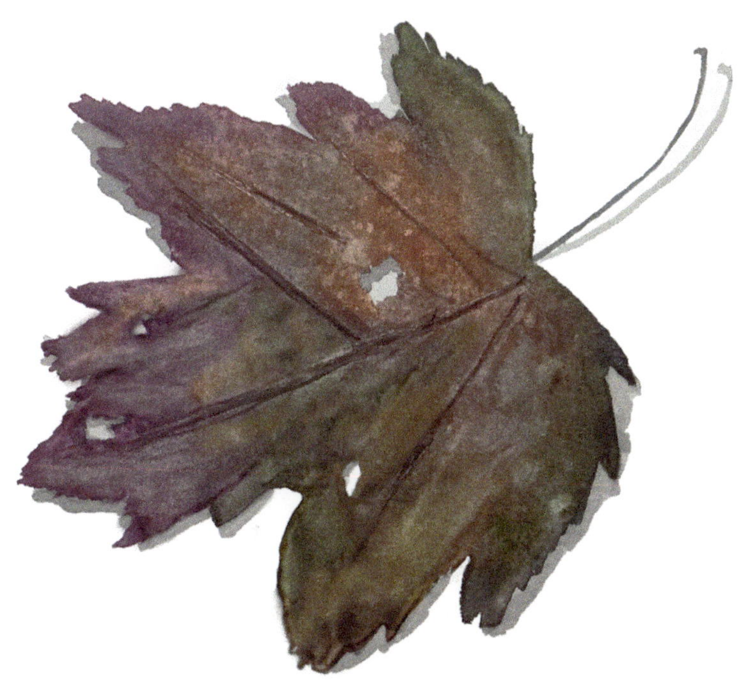

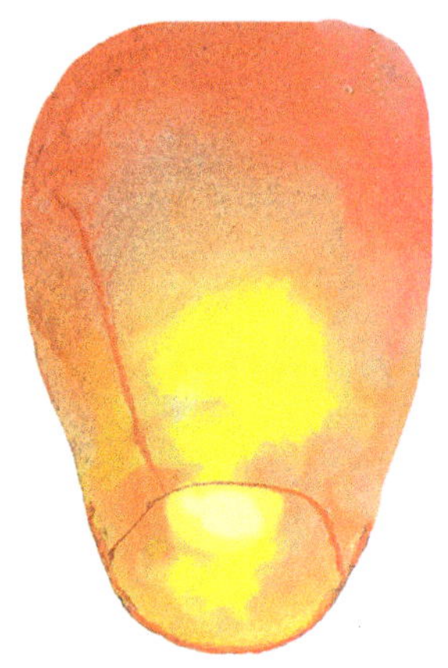

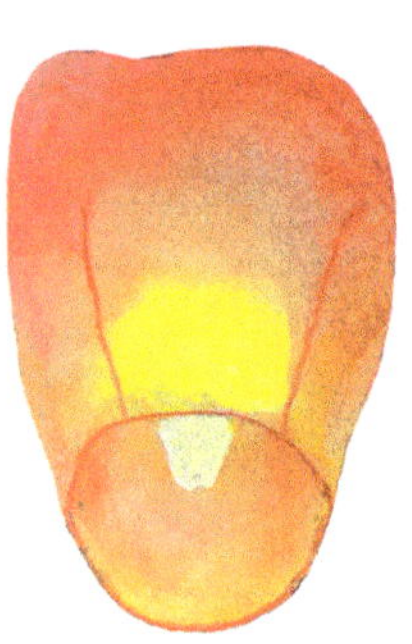

Lightning Source UK Ltd.
Milton Keynes UK
UKHW052220191021
392476UK00003B/21